THIS GUIDE BELONGS TO

....

If lost or stolen please contact me

Mobile Number:..

Email Address:..

Maria Joseph
Achieve: Short Practical Guide to Successful Adulting

All rights reserved
Copyright © 2024 by **Maria Joseph**

Published by Spines
ISBN: 979-8-89383-868-8

CONTENTS

USING THE ACHIEVE GUIDE 4

CREATING AN ANNUAL PLAN 6

BEGINNER GUIDE TO CREATING A HOLISTIC SELF 8

CREATING YOUR PERSONALISED ANNUAL PLAN 10

YEAR AT A GLANCE 12

CREATING YOUR ANNUAL FINANCIAL PLAN 14

FIRST QUARTER (January to March) 16

    Planning January 18

    Planning February 32

    Planning March 44

SECOND QUARTER (April to June) 56

    Planning April 58

    Planning May 70

    Planning June 82

THIRD QUARTER (July to September) 94

    Planning July 96

    Planning August 108

    Planning September 120

FOURTH QUARTER (October to December) 132

    Planning October 134

    Planning November 146

    Planning December 158

BUILDING THE ACHIEVE MINDSET 170

USING THE ACHIEVE GUIDE

CONGRATULATIONS!!! You took the first step toward investing in YOURSELF!

Personal planners are a great and easy way to organise your life and positively influence your time management skills. While it may take some trial and error to determine what works best for you, the habit and routine of planning will definitely enhance your productivity and improve your life! Writing has a positive effect on cognitive development and brain activity. Research indicates that writing by hand helps improve learning and memory and that you are 42% more likely to reach a goal when you write it down.

The Achieve Guide is designed to help you become the very BEST VERSION of yourself through a complete 'Glow Up' (mental, physical, and emotional transformation in readiness for your achievement). Individuals who have experienced transformations of this nature, are often more mature, confident, and feel more attractive. My guide combines all the individual elements of success into a single framework, to help you gradually but permanently shift your priorities toward caring for your best asset, YOURSELF and optimising your most precious resource, YOUR TIME! When you are at your best, then you can achieve the most success.

My guide is designed on the premise that with the right balance of activities, you will achieve optimum performance! I therefore provide space for you to record the following information daily;

● **Gratitude** - Being grateful for past success and current possessions allows us to better navigate adversity. Gratitude makes us more resilient and enables us to attract even more

● **Hydration** - Water consumption increases our energy levels, improves brain function, prevents infections, improves sleep and keeps our organs functioning properly. 8 glasses of water per day is recommended for the average adult

● **Sleep** - A minimum of eight (8) hours sleep reduces stress, boosts our immune system, improves memory and increases productivity

● **Exercise** - Paramount to overall health, fitness and well-being, exercise protects against chronic diseases and improves memory and brain function

● **Diet & Nutrition** - A balanced diet boosts immunity, provides energy and lowers risk of heart disease, type 2 diabetes and some cancers

● **Expenditure** - Although perhaps the most important element of our physical existence as it enables us to pay for all the things required to physically sustain us, it is often overlooked. Once you begin to track exactly how your money is being spent, you can select the areas in which you can curtail spending to save towards your future financial well-being.

Additionally, to be the very best version of yourself, I recommend the adoption of a regular physical, mental, emotional and spiritual Self-Care routine. Please remember that the requirements and frequency of self-care elements will vary from person to person depending on individual needs, lifestyle and personal preferences.

ADDITIONAL FEATURES OF THE ACHIEVE GUIDE

● **Do It Yourself (DIY)** - set personal goals based on individualistic priorities as everyone's idea of success differs

● **Timeless** - allows for the utilisation of every page as pages are not day/date specific

● **Annual Plan Sample Guide** - annual planning made easy by way of a practical easy to understand example

● **Money Mindset Template** - the achievement of every goal and execution of every plan requires money

● **Yearly Overview** - to glance at the entire year in a single view

● **Quarterly Planner** - stay on track by expressing annual goals as quarterly plans

● **Monthly Planner** - for effortless determination of availability when scheduling events and activities

● **Weekly Planner** - take control of your entire week

● **Daily Planner** - some days require more detailed planning than others

● **Habit Trackers** - to build daily positive habits consistently

● **Quarterly Review, Assessment and Feedback Template** - these elements are essential for development

CREATING AN ANNUAL PLAN

"Most people overestimate what they can do in one year and underestimate what they can do in ten years." **BILL GATES**

Set strategic goals for where you see yourself in 10 years, 5 years, 3 years and in one year.

Create an annual plan to take you to your one year milestone marker.

Annual Goals must be **SMART**

Specific - clearly defined or identified

Measureable - capable of being quantified

Achievable - can reasonably be accomplished

Relevant - important and correlates to your larger vision

Time-bound - a set timeline in which to be completed

Each goal must be connected to a timeline (when it will be achieved) and to a budget (how much money is required).

As goals and objectives are always (directly or indirectly) tied to money, setting annual financial goals are an absolute must! Creating an annual financial plan will assist you in adopting the right money mindset necessary for success. Be sure to understand the difference between NEEDS and WANTS. You should know and understand your recurring expenses so that you can plan properly and estimate your projected expenditure with a high level of certainty. You should also start saving for your retirement from the very first day of work at your very first job. Your future retired self will definitely thank you. Additional savings are an absolute must and as unplanned/emergency situations negatively impact your savings, be sure to put aside a budget for emergency situations.

1. Prioritise the things that are most important to YOU.

2. Set a monthly budget and do not cross it. Do not extend yourself beyond your annual goal.

3. Avoid "Emergencies" - Pre-planning will always save you money! Remember that a lack of planning or poor planning will cost you more. Do not allow it to become an emergency factor. For example, if you don't service your vehicle on time and it breaks down, it will always cost more to repair. Avoid that emergency expense, by servicing your vehicle on time.

Once you establish your annual goals, divide them into quarterly goals and then divide your quarterly goals into monthly goals. If you require additional structure, sub-divide your monthly goals into weekly goals and your weekly goals into daily goals. For example if your annual plan includes reading 12 books, your quarterly plan will require you to read 3 books per quarter and one book per month. If you need additional structure, you can divide your monthly book into how many chapters you need to read per week and break that down further into how many pages you need to read a day. This will make the overall goal easier to accomplish. Remember, consistency is the key because drops fill buckets!

In executing your annual plan, be sure to use the monthly planner to assist you in staying abreast of events, engagements and activities to which you are committed. Using the monthly planner will also give you an overview of your month and keep you from double-booking more than one event or activity on the same day at the same time.

Be sure to set aside a couple hours every Sunday to pre-plan your week. Do this by writing in your 'absolutely must achieve goals, events, engagements, meetings and activities'. Be sure to leave enough space and flexibility for the unplanned but important circumstances that will inevitably occur during the week requiring your immediate attention and complete focus. Front loading your week by doing preparatory chores on Sunday (like laundry and meal preparation for the upcoming week), will also ensure that you have more time and energy during the week.

As review, analysis and feedback are crucial for growth and improvement, a template for quarterly review has been included to assist you in understanding the activities that challenge you. Fill out the template in real time (as challenges arise) to have a comprehensive understanding of them when you get to the end of that quarter. This habit will ensure that you are able to address the challenges that plagued you during that quarter and remedy same as you commence the upcoming quarter.

CREATING YOUR BEST SELF

FINANCIAL GOALS

Buy Critical Illness and Life Insurance

Save $12,000

PROFESSIONAL DEVELOPMENT GOALS

Read 6 professional development books

Attend 2 Professional Development Workshops

WORK GOALS

Perfect attendance & punctuality Record

Improve performance appraisal score

PERSONAL DEVELOPMENT GOALS

Engage in Frequent Self Care

Read 6 professional development books

PHYSICAL FITNESS GOALS

Be more active

Lose 20 lbs

SPIRITUAL GOALS

Pray

Community Fellowship (church or other group)

RELATIONSHIP GOALS

Spend more time with your significant other

Take a vacation together

SOCIAL GOALS

Go out more

Make 2 new Friends

GENERAL GROWTH/DEVELOPMENT GOALS

Volunteer to serve the less fortunate

Learn to Dance

EMOTIONAL/INNER CHILD GOALS

Joyful release of Inner child for fun activity

ANY OTHER GOALS

Start a Kitchen Garden

Annual Development Plan (example)

FREQUENCY OR TIMEFRAME BY WHICH TO ACCOMPLISH GOAL	COST/BUDGET & OR RESOURCES REQUIRED
By June 30, YEAR	$450 Monthly
By December 31, YEAR	Save $1000 per month consistently
By December 31, YEAR	$600 + 20 hrs per book
June 30, YEAR & Dec 31, YEAR	$5000
From Jan 1 to December 31	To be determined by each individual
Next performance Appraisal	To be determined by each individual
At least once per week	$200 + 4 hrs per week
By December 31, YEAR	$500 + 20 hrs per book
At least 3 times per week	3 hours per week
By December 31, YEAR	Gym Membership
Daily	20 mins per day
At least once per month	Donations $ + 2 hrs
At least once per week	$250 per date
Second week in June	$10,000
1 outing every fortnight	$150 per outing + 4 hrs
By December 31, YEAR	2 hrs per week
At least once monthly	8 hrs per month
At least once per week	$400 per month + 1 hr per week
Once per Week	$200 + 4 hrs per week
At least once per week	$1500 + 2 hrs weekly

CREATING YOUR PERSONALISED ANNUAL PLAN

ANNUAL GOAL

FREQUENCY OR TIMEFRAME BY WHICH TO ACCOMPLISH GOAL	COST/BUDGET & OR RESOURCES REQUIRED

YEAR AT A GLANCE

	JAN	FEB	MAR	APR	MAY	JUN
1						
2						
3						
4						
5						
6						
7						
8						
9						
10						
11						
12						
13						
14						
15						
16						
17						
18						
19						
20						
21						
22						
23						
24						
25						
26						
27						
28						
29						
30						
31						

JUL	AUG	SEP	OCT	NOV	DEC

CREATING YOUR ANNUAL FINANCIAL PLAN

Year:..

Beginning Net Worth:..

Starting Debt Balance:..

Debt Payoff Goal:..

	PROJECTED INCOME	ACTUAL INCOME	PROJECTED EXPENSES	ACTUAL EXPENSES
January				
February				
March				
1st Quarter Total				
April				
May				
June				
2nd Quarter Total				
July				
August				
September				
3rd Quarter Total				
October				
November				
December				
4th Quarter Total				
ANNUAL TOTAL				

Beginning Net Worth: ....

Income Goal: ....

Saving Goal: ....

Donation Goal: ....

PROJECTED SAVINGS	ACTUAL SAVINGS	PROJECTED DEBT	ACTUAL DEBT

FIRST QUARTER (JANUARY TO MARCH)

JANUARY

FEBRUARY

MARCH

*"Start Where You Are. Use What You Have. Do What You Can." - **Arthur Ashe***

PLANNING JANUARY

NOTES

MONDAY	TUESDAY	WEDNESDAY

THURSDAY	FRIDAY	SATURDAY	SUNDAY

TRACKING YOUR MONTHLY EXPENSES

DATE PAID	EXPENSE

EXPECTED	ACTUAL	DIFFERENCE

PLANNING YOUR WEEK

MONDAY ☐	TUESDAY ☐	WEDNESDAY ☐

THURSDAY ☐	FRIDAY ☐	SATURDAY ☐
		SUNDAY ☐

PLANNING YOUR WEEK

MONDAY	TUESDAY	WEDNESDAY

THURSDAY	FRIDAY	SATURDAY

		SUNDAY

PLANNING YOUR WEEK

MONDAY ☐	TUESDAY ☐	WEDNESDAY ☐

THURSDAY ☐	FRIDAY ☐	SATURDAY ☐
		SUNDAY ☐

PLANNING YOUR WEEK

MONDAY	TUESDAY	WEDNESDAY

THURSDAY	FRIDAY	SATURDAY

SUNDAY

DAILY PLAN

DATE .... S M T W T F S

SCHEDULE

7:00am	
7:30am	
8:00am	
8:30am	
9:00am	
9:30am	
10:00am	
10:30am	
11:00am	
11:30am	
12 noon	
12:30pm	
1:00pm	
1:30pm	
2:00pm	
2:30pm	
3:00pm	

NOTES

TOP PRIORITIES

1
2
3
4
5

GRATITUDE

1
2
3
4
5

TO DO   ✔ OK   ➡ DELAY   ✖ CANCEL

SLEEP DURATION & QUALITY

Hours: Mins:

HEALTH & FITNESS

WATER INTAKE

MEAL TRACKING

EXPENDITURE

 **MOOD TODAY**     

DAILY PLAN

DATE .... S M T W T F S

SCHEDULE

7:00am	
7:30am	
8:00am	
8:30am	
9:00am	
9:30am	
10:00am	
10:30am	
11:00am	
11:30am	
12 noon	
12:30pm	
1:00pm	
1:30pm	
2:00pm	
2:30pm	
3:00pm	

TOP PRIORITIES

1
2
3
4
5

GRATITUDE

1
2
3
4
5

TO DO   ✔ OK   ➡ DELAY   ✖ CANCEL

☐
☐
☐
☐
☐

SLEEP DURATION & QUALITY

Hours: Mins:

HEALTH & FITNESS

WATER INTAKE

MEAL TRACKING

EXPENDITURE

☐
☐
☐
☐
☐

NOTES

MOOD TODAY     

DAILY PLAN

DATE .... S M T W T F S

SCHEDULE

7:00am	
7:30am	
8:00am	
8:30am	
9:00am	
9:30am	
10:00am	
10:30am	
11:00am	
11:30am	
12 noon	
12:30pm	
1:00pm	
1:30pm	
2:00pm	
2:30pm	
3:00pm	

TOP PRIORITIES

1
2
3
4
5

GRATITUDE

1
2
3
4
5

TO DO ✔ OK ➡ DELAY ✖ CANCEL

SLEEP DURATION & QUALITY

Hours: Mins:

HEALTH & FITNESS

WATER INTAKE

NOTES

MEAL TRACKING

EXPENDITURE

MOOD TODAY     

DAILY PLAN

DATE .... S M T W T F S

SCHEDULE

7:00am
7:30am
8:00am
8:30am
9:00am
9:30am
10:00am
10:30am
11:00am
11:30am
12 noon
12:30pm
1:00pm
1:30pm
2:00pm
2:30pm
3:00pm

TOP PRIORITIES

1
2
3
4
5

GRATITUDE

1
2
3
4
5

TO DO   ✔ OK   ➡ DELAY   ✖ CANCEL

SLEEP DURATION & QUALITY

Hours: Mins:

HEALTH & FITNESS

WATER INTAKE

NOTES

MEAL TRACKING

EXPENDITURE

MOOD TODAY     

NOTES

MONDAY	TUESDAY	WEDNESDAY

"Sometimes the smallest step in the right direction ends up being the biggest step of your life. Tip toe if you must, but take the step" - **Naeem Callaway**

THURSDAY	FRIDAY	SATURDAY	SUNDAY

TRACKING YOUR MONTHLY EXPENSES

DATE PAID	EXPENSE
Household Expenses	
	Rent/Mortgage
	Electric
	Water
	Internet
	Cable
	Telephone
Monthly Living Expenses	
	Groceries
	Dining Out and Fast Food
	Travel/Gas
	Household Items
	Personal/Beauty Items
	Entertainment
	Childcare
	Personal allowance
Annual/Long Term Expenses	
	House Insurance
	Car Insurance
	Life Insurance
	Health Insurance
	Emergency Fund
	Savings Fund
	Retirement Fund
	Education Fund
	Vacation Fund
	Gift and Event Fund
Additional, Miscellaneous or One Time Expenses	

	EXPECTED	ACTUAL	DIFFERENCE

PLANNING YOUR WEEK

MONDAY ☐	TUESDAY ☐	WEDNESDAY ☐

THURSDAY ☐	FRIDAY ☐	SATURDAY ☐
		SUNDAY ☐

PLANNING YOUR WEEK

MONDAY ☐	TUESDAY ☐	WEDNESDAY ☐

THURSDAY ☐	FRIDAY ☐	SATURDAY ☐
		SUNDAY ☐

PLANNING YOUR WEEK

MONDAY	TUESDAY	WEDNESDAY

THURSDAY	FRIDAY	SATURDAY
		SUNDAY

MONDAY **TUESDAY** **WEDNESDAY**

THURSDAY **FRIDAY** **SATURDAY**

SUNDAY

DAILY PLAN

DATE .... S M T W T F S

SCHEDULE

7:00am	
7:30am	
8:00am	
8:30am	
9:00am	
9:30am	
10:00am	
10:30am	
11:00am	
11:30am	
12 noon	
12:30pm	
1:00pm	
1:30pm	
2:00pm	
2:30pm	
3:00pm	

TOP PRIORITIES

1
2
3
4
5

GRATITUDE

1
2
3
4
5

TO DO   ✔ OK   ➡ DELAY   ✖ CANCEL

☐
☐
☐
☐
☐

SLEEP DURATION & QUALITY

Hours: Mins:

HEALTH & FITNESS

WATER INTAKE

NOTES

MEAL TRACKING

EXPENDITURE

☐
☐
☐
☐
☐

MOOD TODAY    

DAILY PLAN

DATE .... S M T W T F S

SCHEDULE

7:00am
7:30am
8:00am
8:30am
9:00am
9:30am
10:00am
10:30am
11:00am
11:30am
12 noon
12:30pm
1:00pm
1:30pm
2:00pm
2:30pm
3:00pm

TOP PRIORITIES

1
2
3
4
5

GRATITUDE

1
2
3
4
5

TO DO ✔ OK ➡ DELAY ✖ CANCEL

☐
☐
☐
☐
☐

SLEEP DURATION & QUALITY

Hours: Mins:

HEALTH & FITNESS

WATER INTAKE

NOTES

MEAL TRACKING

EXPENDITURE

☐
☐
☐
☐
☐
☐

MOOD TODAY     

DAILY PLAN

DATE .... S M T W T F S

SCHEDULE

7:00am	
7:30am	
8:00am	
8:30am	
9:00am	
9:30am	
10:00am	
10:30am	
11:00am	
11:30am	
12 noon	
12:30pm	
1:00pm	
1:30pm	
2:00pm	
2:30pm	
3:00pm	

TOP PRIORITIES

1
2
3
4
5

GRATITUDE

1
2
3
4
5

TO DO   ✔ OK   ➡ DELAY   ✖ CANCEL

☐
☐
☐
☐
☐

SLEEP DURATION & QUALITY

Hours: Mins:

HEALTH & FITNESS

WATER INTAKE

MEAL TRACKING

EXPENDITURE

☐
☐
☐
☐
☐

NOTES

MOOD TODAY    

DAILY PLAN

DATE .... S M T W T F S

SCHEDULE

7:00am	
7:30am	
8:00am	
8:30am	
9:00am	
9:30am	
10:00am	
10:30am	
11:00am	
11:30am	
12 noon	
12:30pm	
1:00pm	
1:30pm	
2:00pm	
2:30pm	
3:00pm	

TOP PRIORITIES

1
2
3
4
5

GRATITUDE

1
2
3
4
5

TO DO   ✔ OK   ➡ DELAY   ✖ CANCEL

SLEEP DURATION & QUALITY

Hours: Mins:

HEALTH & FITNESS

WATER INTAKE

NOTES

MEAL TRACKING

EXPENDITURE

MOOD TODAY     

PLANNING MARCH

NOTES

MONDAY	TUESDAY	WEDNESDAY
☐	☐	☐
☐	☐	☐
☐	☐	☐
☐	☐	☐
☐	☐	☐

Wake up every day with the expectation that something amazing is about to happen

THURSDAY	FRIDAY	SATURDAY	SUNDAY

TRACKING YOUR MONTHLY EXPENSES

DATE PAID	EXPENSE
Household Expenses	
	Rent/Mortgage
	Electric
	Water
	Internet
	Cable
	Telephone
Monthly Living Expenses	
	Groceries
	Dining Out and Fast Food
	Travel/Gas
	Household Items
	Personal/Beauty Items
	Entertainment
	Childcare
	Personal allowance
Annual/Long Term Expenses	
	House Insurance
	Car Insurance
	Life Insurance
	Health Insurance
	Emergency Fund
	Savings Fund
	Retirement Fund
	Education Fund
	Vacation Fund
	Gift and Event Fund
Additional, Miscellaneous or One Time Expenses	

Month:...

Income:...

Total Expenses:...

Savings:...

Final Total:...

	EXPECTED	ACTUAL	DIFFERENCE

PLANNING YOUR WEEK

MONDAY	TUESDAY	WEDNESDAY

THURSDAY	FRIDAY	SATURDAY

		SUNDAY

PLANNING YOUR WEEK

MONDAY	TUESDAY	WEDNESDAY

THURSDAY	FRIDAY	SATURDAY

		SUNDAY

PLANNING YOUR WEEK

MONDAY ☐	TUESDAY ☐	WEDNESDAY ☐

THURSDAY ☐	FRIDAY ☐	SATURDAY ☐
		SUNDAY ☐

PLANNING YOUR WEEK

MONDAY	TUESDAY	WEDNESDAY

THURSDAY	FRIDAY	SATURDAY

SUNDAY

DAILY PLAN

DATE .... S M T W T F S

SCHEDULE

7:00am	
7:30am	
8:00am	
8:30am	
9:00am	
9:30am	
10:00am	
10:30am	
11:00am	
11:30am	
12 noon	
12:30pm	
1:00pm	
1:30pm	
2:00pm	
2:30pm	
3:00pm	

TOP PRIORITIES

1
2
3
4
5

GRATITUDE

1
2
3
4
5

TO DO   ✔ OK   ➡ DELAY   ✖ CANCEL

SLEEP DURATION & QUALITY

Hours: Mins:

HEALTH & FITNESS

WATER INTAKE

MEAL TRACKING

EXPENDITURE

NOTES

MOOD TODAY    

DAILY PLAN

DATE .... S M T W T F S

SCHEDULE

| 7:00am |
| 7:30am |
| 8:00am |
| 8:30am |
| 9:00am |
| 9:30am |
| 10:00am |
| 10:30am |
| 11:00am |
| 11:30am |
| 12 noon |
| 12:30pm |
| 1:00pm |
| 1:30pm |
| 2:00pm |
| 2:30pm |
| 3:00pm |

TOP PRIORITIES

1
2
3
4
5

GRATITUDE

1
2
3
4
5

TO DO   ✔ OK   ➡ DELAY   ✖ CANCEL

☐
☐
☐
☐
☐

SLEEP DURATION & QUALITY

Hours: Mins:

HEALTH & FITNESS

WATER INTAKE

NOTES

MEAL TRACKING

EXPENDITURE

☐
☐
☐
☐
☐

MOOD TODAY     

QUARTELY REVIEW ASSESSMENT AND FEEDBACK

ACTIVITY/TASK	DATE ASSIGNED

	DATE COMPLETED	CHALLENGES ENCOUNTERED	MECHANISMS FOR OVERCOMING & AVOIDING FUTURE SIMILAR OCCURRENCES

SECOND QUARTER (APRIL TO JUNE)

"I AM two of the most powerful words for what you put after them shapes your reality" - Bevan Lee

PLANNING APRIL

MONDAY	TUESDAY	WEDNESDAY

"Each day is an adventure in discovering the meaning of life" -
Jack Canfield

THURSDAY	FRIDAY	SATURDAY	SUNDAY

TRACKING YOUR MONTHLY EXPENSES

DATE PAID	EXPENSE
Household Expenses	
	Rent/Mortgage
	Electric
	Water
	Internet
	Cable
	Telephone
Monthly Living Expenses	
	Groceries
	Dining Out and Fast Food
	Travel/Gas
	Household Items
	Personal/Beauty Items
	Entertainment
	Childcare
	Personal allowance
Annual/Long Term Expenses	
	House Insurance
	Car Insurance
	Life Insurance
	Health Insurance
	Emergency Fund
	Savings Fund
	Retirement Fund
	Education Fund
	Vacation Fund
	Gift and Event Fund
Additional, Miscellaneous or One Time Expenses	

Month: ....

Income: ....

Total Expenses: ....

Savings: ....

Final Total: ....

EXPECTED	ACTUAL	DIFFERENCE

PLANNING YOUR WEEK

MONDAY	TUESDAY	WEDNESDAY

THURSDAY	FRIDAY	SATURDAY

		SUNDAY

PLANNING YOUR WEEK

MONDAY	TUESDAY	WEDNESDAY

THURSDAY	FRIDAY	SATURDAY

SUNDAY

PLANNING YOUR WEEK

MONDAY ☐	TUESDAY ☐	WEDNESDAY ☐

THURSDAY ☐	FRIDAY ☐	SATURDAY ☐
		SUNDAY ☐

PLANNING YOUR WEEK

MONDAY ☐	TUESDAY ☐	WEDNESDAY ☐

THURSDAY ☐	FRIDAY ☐	SATURDAY ☐
		SUNDAY ☐

DAILY PLAN

DATE .... S M T W T F S

SCHEDULE

7:00am	
7:30am	
8:00am	
8:30am	
9:00am	
9:30am	
10:00am	
10:30am	
11:00am	
11:30am	
12 noon	
12:30pm	
1:00pm	
1:30pm	
2:00pm	
2:30pm	
3:00pm	

TOP PRIORITIES

1
2
3
4
5

GRATITUDE

1
2
3
4
5

TO DO ✔ OK ➡ DELAY ✖ CANCEL

- [ ]
- [ ]
- [ ]
- [ ]
- [ ]

SLEEP DURATION & QUALITY

Hours: Mins:

HEALTH & FITNESS

WATER INTAKE

MEAL TRACKING

EXPENDITURE

- [ ]
- [ ]
- [ ]
- [ ]
- [ ]

NOTES

 MOOD TODAY     

DAILY PLAN

DATE .... S M T W T F S

SCHEDULE

7:00am	
7:30am	
8:00am	
8:30am	
9:00am	
9:30am	
10:00am	
10:30am	
11:00am	
11:30am	
12 noon	
12:30pm	
1:00pm	
1:30pm	
2:00pm	
2:30pm	
3:00pm	

NOTES

TOP PRIORITIES

1
2
3
4
5

GRATITUDE

1
2
3
4
5

TO DO   ✔ OK   ➡ DELAY   ✖ CANCEL

SLEEP DURATION & QUALITY

Hours: Mins:

HEALTH & FITNESS

WATER INTAKE

MEAL TRACKING

EXPENDITURE

MOOD TODAY    

DAILY PLAN

DATE .... S M T W T F S

SCHEDULE

7:00am	
7:30am	
8:00am	
8:30am	
9:00am	
9:30am	
10:00am	
10:30am	
11:00am	
11:30am	
12 noon	
12:30pm	
1:00pm	
1:30pm	
2:00pm	
2:30pm	
3:00pm	

NOTES

TOP PRIORITIES

1
2
3
4
5

GRATITUDE

1
2
3
4
5

TO DO   ✔ OK   ➡ DELAY   ✖ CANCEL

SLEEP DURATION & QUALITY

Hours: Mins:

HEALTH & FITNESS

WATER INTAKE

MEAL TRACKING

EXPENDITURE

MOOD TODAY    

DAILY PLAN

DATE .... S M T W T F S

SCHEDULE

7:00am	
7:30am	
8:00am	
8:30am	
9:00am	
9:30am	
10:00am	
10:30am	
11:00am	
11:30am	
12 noon	
12:30pm	
1:00pm	
1:30pm	
2:00pm	
2:30pm	
3:00pm	

NOTES

TOP PRIORITIES

1
2
3
4
5

GRATITUDE

1
2
3
4
5

TO DO ✔ OK ➡ DELAY ✖ CANCEL

SLEEP DURATION & QUALITY

Hours: Mins:

HEALTH & FITNESS

WATER INTAKE

MEAL TRACKING

EXPENDITURE

MOOD TODAY     

PLANNING MAY

NOTES

MONDAY	TUESDAY	WEDNESDAY

THURSDAY	FRIDAY	SATURDAY	SUNDAY

TRACKING YOUR MONTHLY EXPENSES

DATE PAID	EXPENSE
Household Expenses	
	Rent/Mortgage
	Electric
	Water
	Internet
	Cable
	Telephone
Monthly Living Expenses	
	Groceries
	Dining Out and Fast Food
	Travel/Gas
	Household Items
	Personal/Beauty Items
	Entertainment
	Childcare
	Personal allowance
Annual/Long Term Expenses	
	House Insurance
	Car Insurance
	Life Insurance
	Health Insurance
	Emergency Fund
	Savings Fund
	Retirement Fund
	Education Fund
	Vacation Fund
	Gift and Event Fund
Additional, Miscellaneous or One Time Expenses	

Month: ....

Income: ....

Total Expenses: ....

Savings: ....

Final Total: ....

	EXPECTED	ACTUAL	DIFFERENCE

PLANNING YOUR WEEK

MONDAY	TUESDAY	WEDNESDAY

THURSDAY	FRIDAY	SATURDAY

		SUNDAY

PLANNING YOUR WEEK

MONDAY	TUESDAY	WEDNESDAY

THURSDAY	FRIDAY	SATURDAY

SUNDAY

PLANNING YOUR WEEK

MONDAY ☐	TUESDAY ☐	WEDNESDAY ☐

THURSDAY ☐	FRIDAY ☐	SATURDAY ☐
		SUNDAY ☐

PLANNING YOUR WEEK

MONDAY	TUESDAY	WEDNESDAY

THURSDAY	FRIDAY	SATURDAY
		SUNDAY

DAILY PLAN

DATE .... S M T W T F S

SCHEDULE

| 7:00am |
| 7:30am |
| 8:00am |
| 8:30am |
| 9:00am |
| 9:30am |
| 10:00am |
| 10:30am |
| 11:00am |
| 11:30am |
| 12 noon |
| 12:30pm |
| 1:00pm |
| 1:30pm |
| 2:00pm |
| 2:30pm |
| 3:00pm |

TOP PRIORITIES

1
2
3
4
5

GRATITUDE

1
2
3
4
5

TO DO ✔ OK ➡ DELAY ✖ CANCEL

SLEEP DURATION & QUALITY

Hours: Mins:

HEALTH & FITNESS

NOTES

WATER INTAKE

MEAL TRACKING

EXPENDITURE

MOOD TODAY   

DAILY PLAN

DATE .... S M T W T F S

SCHEDULE

| 7:00am |
| 7:30am |
| 8:00am |
| 8:30am |
| 9:00am |
| 9:30am |
| 10:00am |
| 10:30am |
| 11:00am |
| 11:30am |
| 12 noon |
| 12:30pm |
| 1:00pm |
| 1:30pm |
| 2:00pm |
| 2:30pm |
| 3:00pm |

TOP PRIORITIES

1
2
3
4
5

GRATITUDE

1
2
3
4
5

TO DO   ✔ OK   ➡ DELAY   ✖ CANCEL

SLEEP DURATION & QUALITY

Hours: Mins:

HEALTH & FITNESS

WATER INTAKE

MEAL TRACKING

EXPENDITURE

NOTES

MOOD TODAY     

DAILY PLAN

DATE .... S M T W T F S

SCHEDULE

7:00am	
7:30am	
8:00am	
8:30am	
9:00am	
9:30am	
10:00am	
10:30am	
11:00am	
11:30am	
12 noon	
12:30pm	
1:00pm	
1:30pm	
2:00pm	
2:30pm	
3:00pm	

TOP PRIORITIES

1
2
3
4
5

GRATITUDE

1
2
3
4
5

TO DO ✔ OK ➡ DELAY ✖ CANCEL

☐
☐
☐
☐
☐

SLEEP DURATION & QUALITY

Hours: Mins:

HEALTH & FITNESS

WATER INTAKE

MEAL TRACKING

EXPENDITURE

☐
☐
☐
☐
☐

NOTES

MOOD TODAY     

DAILY PLAN

DATE .... S M T W T F S

SCHEDULE

| 7:00am |
| 7:30am |
| 8:00am |
| 8:30am |
| 9:00am |
| 9:30am |
| 10:00am |
| 10:30am |
| 11:00am |
| 11:30am |
| 12 noon |
| 12:30pm |
| 1:00pm |
| 1:30pm |
| 2:00pm |
| 2:30pm |
| 3:00pm |

TOP PRIORITIES

1
2
3
4
5

GRATITUDE

1
2
3
4
5

TO DO   ✔ OK   ➡ DELAY   ✖ CANCEL

☐
☐
☐
☐
☐

SLEEP DURATION & QUALITY

Hours: Mins:

HEALTH & FITNESS

WATER INTAKE

MEAL TRACKING

EXPENDITURE

☐
☐
☐
☐
☐

NOTES

MOOD TODAY    

PLANNING JUNE

NOTES

MONDAY	TUESDAY	WEDNESDAY

Be grateful for every second of every day you get to spend with people you love -
Mandy Hale

THURSDAY	FRIDAY	SATURDAY	SUNDAY

TRACKING YOUR MONTHLY EXPENSES

DATE PAID	EXPENSE
Household Expenses	
	Rent/Mortgage
	Electric
	Water
	Internet
	Cable
	Telephone
Monthly Living Expenses	
	Groceries
	Dining Out and Fast Food
	Travel/Gas
	Household Items
	Personal/Beauty Items
	Entertainment
	Childcare
	Personal allowance
Annual/Long Term Expenses	
	House Insurance
	Car Insurance
	Life Insurance
	Health Insurance
	Emergency Fund
	Savings Fund
	Retirement Fund
	Education Fund
	Vacation Fund
	Gift and Event Fund
Additional, Miscellaneous or One Time Expenses	

Month: ....

Income: ....

Total Expenses: ....

Savings: ....

Final Total: ....

	EXPECTED	ACTUAL	DIFFERENCE

PLANNING YOUR WEEK

MONDAY	TUESDAY	WEDNESDAY

THURSDAY	FRIDAY	SATURDAY

SUNDAY

PLANNING YOUR WEEK

MONDAY ☐	TUESDAY ☐	WEDNESDAY ☐

THURSDAY ☐	FRIDAY ☐	SATURDAY ☐
		SUNDAY ☐

PLANNING YOUR WEEK

MONDAY ☐	TUESDAY ☐	WEDNESDAY ☐

THURSDAY ☐	FRIDAY ☐	SATURDAY ☐
		SUNDAY ☐

PLANNING YOUR WEEK

MONDAY ☐	TUESDAY ☐	WEDNESDAY ☐

THURSDAY ☐	FRIDAY ☐	SATURDAY ☐
		SUNDAY ☐

DAILY PLAN

DATE .... S M T W T F S

SCHEDULE

7:00am	
7:30am	
8:00am	
8:30am	
9:00am	
9:30am	
10:00am	
10:30am	
11:00am	
11:30am	
12 noon	
12:30pm	
1:00pm	
1:30pm	
2:00pm	
2:30pm	
3:00pm	

TOP PRIORITIES

1
2
3
4
5

GRATITUDE

1
2
3
4
5

TO DO   ✔ OK   ➡ DELAY   ✖ CANCEL

☐
☐
☐
☐
☐

SLEEP DURATION & QUALITY

Hours: Mins:

HEALTH & FITNESS

WATER INTAKE

MEAL TRACKING

EXPENDITURE

☐
☐
☐
☐
☐

NOTES

MOOD TODAY     

DAILY PLAN

DATE .... S M T W T F S

SCHEDULE

| 7:00am |
| 7:30am |
| 8:00am |
| 8:30am |
| 9:00am |
| 9:30am |
| 10:00am |
| 10:30am |
| 11:00am |
| 11:30am |
| 12 noon |
| 12:30pm |
| 1:00pm |
| 1:30pm |
| 2:00pm |
| 2:30pm |
| 3:00pm |

TOP PRIORITIES

1
2
3
4
5

GRATITUDE

1
2
3
4
5

TO DO   ✔ OK   ➡ DELAY   ✖ CANCEL

SLEEP DURATION & QUALITY

Hours: Mins:

HEALTH & FITNESS

WATER INTAKE

NOTES

MEAL TRACKING

EXPENDITURE

MOOD TODAY     

QUARTELY REVIEW ASSESSMENT AND FEEDBACK

ACTIVITY/TASK	DATE ASSIGNED

DATE COMPLETED	CHALLENGES ENCOUNTERED	MECHANISMS FOR OVERCOMING & AVOIDING FUTURE SIMILAR OCCURRENCES

THIRD QUARTER (JULY TO SEPTEMBER)

JULY

AUGUST

SEPTEMBER

PLANNING JULY

NOTES

MONDAY	TUESDAY	WEDNESDAY

THURSDAY	FRIDAY	SATURDAY	SUNDAY

TRACKING YOUR MONTHLY EXPENSES

DATE PAID	EXPENSE
Household Expenses	
	Rent/Mortgage
	Electric
	Water
	Internet
	Cable
	Telephone
Monthly Living Expenses	
	Groceries
	Dining Out and Fast Food
	Travel/Gas
	Household Items
	Personal/Beauty Items
	Entertainment
	Childcare
	Personal allowance
Annual/Long Term Expenses	
	House Insurance
	Car Insurance
	Life Insurance
	Health Insurance
	Emergency Fund
	Savings Fund
	Retirement Fund
	Education Fund
	Vacation Fund
	Gift and Event Fund
Additional, Miscellaneous or One Time Expenses	

Month:...
Income:...
Total Expenses:...
Savings:...
Final Total:...

	EXPECTED	ACTUAL	DIFFERENCE

PLANNING YOUR WEEK

MONDAY	TUESDAY	WEDNESDAY

THURSDAY	FRIDAY	SATURDAY
		SUNDAY

PLANNING YOUR WEEK

MONDAY ☐	TUESDAY ☐	WEDNESDAY ☐

THURSDAY ☐	FRIDAY ☐	SATURDAY ☐
		SUNDAY ☐

PLANNING YOUR WEEK

MONDAY ☐	TUESDAY ☐	WEDNESDAY ☐

THURSDAY ☐	FRIDAY ☐	SATURDAY ☐
		SUNDAY ☐

PLANNING YOUR WEEK

MONDAY	**TUESDAY**	**WEDNESDAY**

THURSDAY	**FRIDAY**	**SATURDAY**
		SUNDAY

DAILY PLAN

DATE .... S M T W T F S

SCHEDULE

7:00am	
7:30am	
8:00am	
8:30am	
9:00am	
9:30am	
10:00am	
10:30am	
11:00am	
11:30am	
12 noon	
12:30pm	
1:00pm	
1:30pm	
2:00pm	
2:30pm	
3:00pm	

TOP PRIORITIES

1
2
3
4
5

GRATITUDE

1
2
3
4
5

TO DO   ✔ OK   ➡ DELAY   ✖ CANCEL

☐
☐
☐
☐
☐

SLEEP DURATION & QUALITY

Hours: Mins:

HEALTH & FITNESS

WATER INTAKE

MEAL TRACKING

EXPENDITURE

☐
☐
☐
☐
☐

NOTES

MOOD TODAY    

DAILY PLAN

DATE .... S M T W T F S

SCHEDULE

7:00am
7:30am
8:00am
8:30am
9:00am
9:30am
10:00am
10:30am
11:00am
11:30am
12 noon
12:30pm
1:00pm
1:30pm
2:00pm
2:30pm
3:00pm

TOP PRIORITIES

1
2
3
4
5

GRATITUDE

1
2
3
4
5

TO DO   ✔ OK   ➡ DELAY   ✖ CANCEL

- [ ]
- [ ]
- [ ]
- [ ]
- [ ]

SLEEP DURATION & QUALITY

Hours: Mins:

HEALTH & FITNESS

WATER INTAKE

MEAL TRACKING

EXPENDITURE

- [ ]
- [ ]
- [ ]
- [ ]
- [ ]

NOTES

MOOD TODAY     

DAILY PLAN

DATE .... S M T W T F S

SCHEDULE

7:00am	
7:30am	
8:00am	
8:30am	
9:00am	
9:30am	
10:00am	
10:30am	
11:00am	
11:30am	
12 noon	
12:30pm	
1:00pm	
1:30pm	
2:00pm	
2:30pm	
3:00pm	

NOTES

TOP PRIORITIES

1
2
3
4
5

GRATITUDE

1
2
3
4
5

TO DO   ✔ OK   ➡ DELAY   ✖ CANCEL

SLEEP DURATION & QUALITY

Hours: Mins:

HEALTH & FITNESS

WATER INTAKE

MEAL TRACKING

EXPENDITURE

MOOD TODAY    

DAILY PLAN

DATE .... S M T W T F S

SCHEDULE

| 7:00am |
| 7:30am |
| 8:00am |
| 8:30am |
| 9:00am |
| 9:30am |
| 10:00am |
| 10:30am |
| 11:00am |
| 11:30am |
| 12 noon |
| 12:30pm |
| 1:00pm |
| 1:30pm |
| 2:00pm |
| 2:30pm |
| 3:00pm |

NOTES

TOP PRIORITIES

1
2
3
4
5

GRATITUDE

1
2
3
4
5

TO DO — ✔ OK ➡ DELAY ✖ CANCEL

SLEEP DURATION & QUALITY

Hours: Mins:

HEALTH & FITNESS

WATER INTAKE

MEAL TRACKING

EXPENDITURE

MOOD TODAY     

PLANNING AUGUST

NOTES

MONDAY	TUESDAY	WEDNESDAY

THURSDAY	FRIDAY	SATURDAY	SUNDAY

TRACKING YOUR MONTHLY EXPENSES

DATE PAID	EXPENSE
Household Expenses	
	Rent/Mortgage
	Electric
	Water
	Internet
	Cable
	Telephone
Monthly Living Expenses	
	Groceries
	Dining Out and Fast Food
	Travel/Gas
	Household Items
	Personal/Beauty Items
	Entertainment
	Childcare
	Personal allowance
Annual/Long Term Expenses	
	House Insurance
	Car Insurance
	Life Insurance
	Health Insurance
	Emergency Fund
	Savings Fund
	Retirement Fund
	Education Fund
	Vacation Fund
	Gift and Event Fund
Additional, Miscellaneous or One Time Expenses	

Month: ....

Income: ....

Total Expenses: ....

Savings: ....

Final Total: ....

	EXPECTED	ACTUAL	DIFFERENCE

PLANNING YOUR WEEK

MONDAY	TUESDAY	WEDNESDAY

THURSDAY	FRIDAY	SATURDAY

SUNDAY

PLANNING YOUR WEEK

MONDAY	TUESDAY	WEDNESDAY

THURSDAY	FRIDAY	SATURDAY
		SUNDAY

PLANNING YOUR WEEK

MONDAY ☐	TUESDAY ☐	WEDNESDAY ☐

THURSDAY ☐	FRIDAY ☐	SATURDAY ☐
		SUNDAY ☐

PLANNING YOUR WEEK

MONDAY ☐	TUESDAY ☐	WEDNESDAY ☐

THURSDAY ☐	FRIDAY ☐	SATURDAY ☐
		SUNDAY ☐

DAILY PLAN

DATE .... S M T W T F S

SCHEDULE

| 7:00am |
| 7:30am |
| 8:00am |
| 8:30am |
| 9:00am |
| 9:30am |
| 10:00am |
| 10:30am |
| 11:00am |
| 11:30am |
| 12 noon |
| 12:30pm |
| 1:00pm |
| 1:30pm |
| 2:00pm |
| 2:30pm |
| 3:00pm |

TOP PRIORITIES

1
2
3
4
5

GRATITUDE

1
2
3
4
5

TO DO   ✔ OK   ➡ DELAY   ✖ CANCEL

SLEEP DURATION & QUALITY

Hours: Mins:

HEALTH & FITNESS

WATER INTAKE

MEAL TRACKING

EXPENDITURE

NOTES

MOOD TODAY    

DAILY PLAN

DATE .... S M T W T F S

SCHEDULE

| 7:00am |
| 7:30am |
| 8:00am |
| 8:30am |
| 9:00am |
| 9:30am |
| 10:00am |
| 10:30am |
| 11:00am |
| 11:30am |
| 12 noon |
| 12:30pm |
| 1:00pm |
| 1:30pm |
| 2:00pm |
| 2:30pm |
| 3:00pm |

TOP PRIORITIES

1
2
3
4
5

GRATITUDE

1
2
3
4
5

TO DO ☑ OK ➡ DELAY ✖ CANCEL

SLEEP DURATION & QUALITY

Hours: Mins:

HEALTH & FITNESS

WATER INTAKE

MEAL TRACKING

EXPENDITURE

NOTES

MOOD TODAY     

DAILY PLAN

DATE .... S M T W T F S

SCHEDULE

| 7:00am |
| 7:30am |
| 8:00am |
| 8:30am |
| 9:00am |
| 9:30am |
| 10:00am |
| 10:30am |
| 11:00am |
| 11:30am |
| 12 noon |
| 12:30pm |
| 1:00pm |
| 1:30pm |
| 2:00pm |
| 2:30pm |
| 3:00pm |

TOP PRIORITIES

1
2
3
4
5

GRATITUDE

1
2
3
4
5

TO DO   ✔ OK   ➡ DELAY   ✖ CANCEL

SLEEP DURATION & QUALITY

Hours: Mins:

HEALTH & FITNESS

WATER INTAKE

NOTES

MEAL TRACKING

EXPENDITURE

MOOD TODAY     

DAILY PLAN

DATE .... S M T W T F S

SCHEDULE

7:00am	
7:30am	
8:00am	
8:30am	
9:00am	
9:30am	
10:00am	
10:30am	
11:00am	
11:30am	
12 noon	
12:30pm	
1:00pm	
1:30pm	
2:00pm	
2:30pm	
3:00pm	

TOP PRIORITIES

1
2
3
4
5

GRATITUDE

1
2
3
4
5

TO DO   ✔ OK   ➡ DELAY   ✖ CANCEL

SLEEP DURATION & QUALITY

Hours: Mins:

HEALTH & FITNESS

WATER INTAKE

MEAL TRACKING

EXPENDITURE

NOTES

MOOD TODAY     

PLANNING SEPTEMBER

NOTES

MONDAY	TUESDAY	WEDNESDAY

THURSDAY	FRIDAY	SATURDAY	SUNDAY
☐	☐	☐	☐
☐	☐	☐	☐
☐	☐	☐	☐
☐	☐	☐	☐
☐	☐	☐	☐

TRACKING YOUR MONTHLY EXPENSES

DATE PAID	EXPENSE
Household Expenses	
	Rent/Mortgage
	Electric
	Water
	Internet
	Cable
	Telephone
Monthly Living Expenses	
	Groceries
	Dining Out and Fast Food
	Travel/Gas
	Household Items
	Personal/Beauty Items
	Entertainment
	Childcare
	Personal allowance
Annual/Long Term Expenses	
	House Insurance
	Car Insurance
	Life Insurance
	Health Insurance
	Emergency Fund
	Savings Fund
	Retirement Fund
	Education Fund
	Vacation Fund
	Gift and Event Fund
Additional, Miscellaneous or One Time Expenses	

Month: ....

Income: ....

Total Expenses: ....

Savings: ....

Final Total: ....

	EXPECTED	ACTUAL	DIFFERENCE

PLANNING YOUR WEEK

MONDAY	TUESDAY	WEDNESDAY

THURSDAY	FRIDAY	SATURDAY
		SUNDAY

PLANNING YOUR WEEK

MONDAY ☐	TUESDAY ☐	WEDNESDAY ☐

THURSDAY ☐	FRIDAY ☐	SATURDAY ☐
		SUNDAY ☐

MONDAY	☐	TUESDAY	☐	WEDNESDAY	☐

THURSDAY	☐	FRIDAY	☐	SATURDAY	☐

				SUNDAY	☐

PLANNING YOUR WEEK

MONDAY ☐	TUESDAY ☐	WEDNESDAY ☐

THURSDAY ☐	FRIDAY ☐	SATURDAY ☐
		SUNDAY ☐

DAILY PLAN

DATE .... S M T W T F S

SCHEDULE

7:00am	
7:30am	
8:00am	
8:30am	
9:00am	
9:30am	
10:00am	
10:30am	
11:00am	
11:30am	
12 noon	
12:30pm	
1:00pm	
1:30pm	
2:00pm	
2:30pm	
3:00pm	

TOP PRIORITIES

1
2
3
4
5

GRATITUDE

1
2
3
4
5

TO DO   ✔ OK   ➡ DELAY   ✖ CANCEL

SLEEP DURATION & QUALITY

Hours: Mins:

HEALTH & FITNESS

WATER INTAKE

MEAL TRACKING

EXPENDITURE

NOTES

MOOD TODAY    

DAILY PLAN

DATE .... S M T W T F S

SCHEDULE

7:00am	
7:30am	
8:00am	
8:30am	
9:00am	
9:30am	
10:00am	
10:30am	
11:00am	
11:30am	
12 noon	
12:30pm	
1:00pm	
1:30pm	
2:00pm	
2:30pm	
3:00pm	

TOP PRIORITIES

1
2
3
4
5

GRATITUDE

1
2
3
4
5

TO DO   ✔ OK   ➡ DELAY   ✖ CANCEL

- [ ]
- [ ]
- [ ]
- [ ]
- [ ]

SLEEP DURATION & QUALITY

Hours: Mins:

HEALTH & FITNESS

NOTES

WATER INTAKE

MEAL TRACKING

EXPENDITURE

- [ ]
- [ ]
- [ ]
- [ ]
- [ ]

MOOD TODAY

QUARTELY REVIEW ASSESSMENT AND FEEDBACK

ACTIVITY/TASK	DATE ASSIGNED

	DATE COMPLETED	CHALLENGES ENCOUNTERED	MECHANISMS FOR OVERCOMING & AVOIDING FUTURE SIMILAR OCCURRENCES

FOURTH QUARTER (OCTOBER TO DECEMBER)

OCTOBER

NOVEMBER

DECEMBER

Let people make incorrect assumptions about you, understand that their narrative has nothing to do with you, but is fuelled by their own fears and insecurities!

PLANNING OCTOBER

NOTES

MONDAY	TUESDAY	WEDNESDAY

THURSDAY	FRIDAY	SATURDAY	SUNDAY

TRACKING YOUR MONTHLY EXPENSES

DATE PAID	EXPENSE
Household Expenses	
	Rent/Mortgage
	Electric
	Water
	Internet
	Cable
	Telephone
Monthly Living Expenses	
	Groceries
	Dining Out and Fast Food
	Travel/Gas
	Household Items
	Personal/Beauty Items
	Entertainment
	Childcare
	Personal allowance
Annual/Long Term Expenses	
	House Insurance
	Car Insurance
	Life Insurance
	Health Insurance
	Emergency Fund
	Savings Fund
	Retirement Fund
	Education Fund
	Vacation Fund
	Gift and Event Fund
Additional, Miscellaneous or One Time Expenses	

Month: ....

Income: ....

Total Expenses: ....

Savings: ....

Final Total: ....

	EXPECTED	ACTUAL	DIFFERENCE

PLANNING YOUR WEEK

MONDAY	TUESDAY	WEDNESDAY

THURSDAY	FRIDAY	SATURDAY

		SUNDAY

PLANNING YOUR WEEK

MONDAY ☐	TUESDAY ☐	WEDNESDAY ☐

THURSDAY ☐	FRIDAY ☐	SATURDAY ☐
		SUNDAY ☐

PLANNING YOUR WEEK

MONDAY	TUESDAY	WEDNESDAY

THURSDAY	FRIDAY	SATURDAY

SUNDAY

PLANNING YOUR WEEK

MONDAY	TUESDAY	WEDNESDAY

THURSDAY	FRIDAY	SATURDAY

		SUNDAY

DAILY PLAN

DATE .... S M T W T F S

SCHEDULE

7:00am
7:30am
8:00am
8:30am
9:00am
9:30am
10:00am
10:30am
11:00am
11:30am
12 noon
12:30pm
1:00pm
1:30pm
2:00pm
2:30pm
3:00pm

TOP PRIORITIES

1
2
3
4
5

GRATITUDE

1
2
3
4
5

TO DO   ✔ OK   ➡ DELAY   ✖ CANCEL

SLEEP DURATION & QUALITY

Hours: Mins:

HEALTH & FITNESS

WATER INTAKE

NOTES

MEAL TRACKING

EXPENDITURE

MOOD TODAY     

DAILY PLAN

DATE .... S M T W T F S

SCHEDULE

7:00am	
7:30am	
8:00am	
8:30am	
9:00am	
9:30am	
10:00am	
10:30am	
11:00am	
11:30am	
12 noon	
12:30pm	
1:00pm	
1:30pm	
2:00pm	
2:30pm	
3:00pm	

TOP PRIORITIES

1
2
3
4
5

GRATITUDE

1
2
3
4
5

TO DO   ✔ OK   ➡ DELAY   ✖ CANCEL

☐
☐
☐
☐
☐

SLEEP DURATION & QUALITY

Hours: Mins:

HEALTH & FITNESS

WATER INTAKE

MEAL TRACKING

EXPENDITURE

☐
☐
☐
☐
☐

NOTES

MOOD TODAY     

DAILY PLAN

DATE .... S M T W T F S

SCHEDULE

7:00am	
7:30am	
8:00am	
8:30am	
9:00am	
9:30am	
10:00am	
10:30am	
11:00am	
11:30am	
12 noon	
12:30pm	
1:00pm	
1:30pm	
2:00pm	
2:30pm	
3:00pm	

TOP PRIORITIES

1
2
3
4
5

GRATITUDE

1
2
3
4
5

TO DO ✔ OK ➡ DELAY ✖ CANCEL

☐
☐
☐
☐
☐

SLEEP DURATION & QUALITY

Hours: Mins:

HEALTH & FITNESS

NOTES

WATER INTAKE

MEAL TRACKING

EXPENDITURE

☐
☐
☐
☐
☐

MOOD TODAY    

DAILY PLAN

DATE .... S M T W T F S

SCHEDULE

7:00am	
7:30am	
8:00am	
8:30am	
9:00am	
9:30am	
10:00am	
10:30am	
11:00am	
11:30am	
12 noon	
12:30pm	
1:00pm	
1:30pm	
2:00pm	
2:30pm	
3:00pm	

TOP PRIORITIES

1
2
3
4
5

GRATITUDE

1
2
3
4
5

TO DO   ✔ OK   ➡ DELAY   ✖ CANCEL

SLEEP DURATION & QUALITY

Hours: Mins:

HEALTH & FITNESS

WATER INTAKE

MEAL TRACKING

EXPENDITURE

NOTES

MOOD TODAY    

PLANNING NOVEMBER

NOTES

MONDAY	TUESDAY	WEDNESDAY

THURSDAY	FRIDAY	SATURDAY	SUNDAY

TRACKING YOUR MONTHLY EXPENSES

DATE PAID	EXPENSE
Household Expenses	
	Rent/Mortgage
	Electric
	Water
	Internet
	Cable
	Telephone
Monthly Living Expenses	
	Groceries
	Dining Out and Fast Food
	Travel/Gas
	Household Items
	Personal/Beauty Items
	Entertainment
	Childcare
	Personal allowance
Annual/Long Term Expenses	
	House Insurance
	Car Insurance
	Life Insurance
	Health Insurance
	Emergency Fund
	Savings Fund
	Retirement Fund
	Education Fund
	Vacation Fund
	Gift and Event Fund
Additional, Miscellaneous or One Time Expenses	

Month:..

Income:..

Total Expenses:..

Savings:...

Final Total:..

	EXPECTED	ACTUAL	DIFFERENCE

PLANNING YOUR WEEK

MONDAY	TUESDAY	WEDNESDAY

THURSDAY	FRIDAY	SATURDAY
		SUNDAY

PLANNING YOUR WEEK

MONDAY	TUESDAY	WEDNESDAY

THURSDAY	FRIDAY	SATURDAY
		SUNDAY

PLANNING YOUR WEEK

MONDAY ☐	TUESDAY ☐	WEDNESDAY ☐

THURSDAY ☐	FRIDAY ☐	SATURDAY ☐
		SUNDAY ☐

PLANNING YOUR WEEK

MONDAY ☐	TUESDAY ☐	WEDNESDAY ☐

THURSDAY ☐	FRIDAY ☐	SATURDAY ☐
		SUNDAY ☐

DAILY PLAN

DATE .... S M T W T F S

SCHEDULE

7:00am	
7:30am	
8:00am	
8:30am	
9:00am	
9:30am	
10:00am	
10:30am	
11:00am	
11:30am	
12 noon	
12:30pm	
1:00pm	
1:30pm	
2:00pm	
2:30pm	
3:00pm	

TOP PRIORITIES

1
2
3
4
5

GRATITUDE

1
2
3
4
5

TO DO   ✔ OK   ➡ DELAY   ✖ CANCEL

- ☐
- ☐
- ☐
- ☐
- ☐

SLEEP DURATION & QUALITY

Hours: Mins:

HEALTH & FITNESS

WATER INTAKE

MEAL TRACKING

EXPENDITURE

- ☐
- ☐
- ☐
- ☐
- ☐

NOTES

MOOD TODAY    

DAILY PLAN

DATE .... S M T W T F S

SCHEDULE

7:00am	
7:30am	
8:00am	
8:30am	
9:00am	
9:30am	
10:00am	
10:30am	
11:00am	
11:30am	
12 noon	
12:30pm	
1:00pm	
1:30pm	
2:00pm	
2:30pm	
3:00pm	

TOP PRIORITIES

1
2
3
4
5

GRATITUDE

1
2
3
4
5

TO DO   ✔ OK   ➡ DELAY   ✖ CANCEL

☐
☐
☐
☐
☐

SLEEP DURATION & QUALITY

Hours: Mins:

HEALTH & FITNESS

WATER INTAKE

MEAL TRACKING

EXPENDITURE

☐
☐
☐
☐
☐

NOTES

MOOD TODAY     

DAILY PLAN

DATE .... S M T W T F S

SCHEDULE

7:00am	
7:30am	
8:00am	
8:30am	
9:00am	
9:30am	
10:00am	
10:30am	
11:00am	
11:30am	
12 noon	
12:30pm	
1:00pm	
1:30pm	
2:00pm	
2:30pm	
3:00pm	

NOTES

TOP PRIORITIES

1
2
3
4
5

GRATITUDE

1
2
3
4
5

TO DO   ✔ OK   ➡ DELAY   ✖ CANCEL

SLEEP DURATION & QUALITY

Hours: Mins:

HEALTH & FITNESS

WATER INTAKE

MEAL TRACKING

EXPENDITURE

MOOD TODAY    

DAILY PLAN

DATE .... S M T W T F S

SCHEDULE

7:00am
7:30am
8:00am
8:30am
9:00am
9:30am
10:00am
10:30am
11:00am
11:30am
12 noon
12:30pm
1:00pm
1:30pm
2:00pm
2:30pm
3:00pm

TOP PRIORITIES

1
2
3
4
5

GRATITUDE

1
2
3
4
5

TO DO   ✔ OK   ➡ DELAY   ✖ CANCEL

SLEEP DURATION & QUALITY

Hours: Mins:

HEALTH & FITNESS

WATER INTAKE

NOTES

MEAL TRACKING

EXPENDITURE

MOOD TODAY     

PLANNING DECEMBER

NOTES

MONDAY	TUESDAY	WEDNESDAY

THURSDAY	FRIDAY	SATURDAY	SUNDAY

TRACKING YOUR MONTHLY EXPENSES

DATE PAID	EXPENSE
Household Expenses	
	Rent/Mortgage
	Electric
	Water
	Internet
	Cable
	Telephone
Monthly Living Expenses	
	Groceries
	Dining Out and Fast Food
	Travel/Gas
	Household Items
	Personal/Beauty Items
	Entertainment
	Childcare
	Personal allowance
Annual/Long Term Expenses	
	House Insurance
	Car Insurance
	Life Insurance
	Health Insurance
	Emergency Fund
	Savings Fund
	Retirement Fund
	Education Fund
	Vacation Fund
	Gift and Event Fund
Additional, Miscellaneous or One Time Expenses	

Month:...

Income:..

Total Expenses:...

Savings:..

Final Total:...

EXPECTED	ACTUAL	DIFFERENCE

PLANNING YOUR WEEK

MONDAY ☐	TUESDAY ☐	WEDNESDAY ☐

THURSDAY ☐	FRIDAY ☐	SATURDAY ☐
		SUNDAY ☐

MONDAY ☐	TUESDAY ☐	WEDNESDAY ☐

THURSDAY ☐	FRIDAY ☐	SATURDAY ☐
		SUNDAY ☐

PLANNING YOUR WEEK

| MONDAY | ☐ | TUESDAY | ☐ | WEDNESDAY | ☐ |

| THURSDAY | ☐ | FRIDAY | ☐ | SATURDAY | ☐ |

| SUNDAY | ☐ |

PLANNING YOUR WEEK

MONDAY	TUESDAY	WEDNESDAY

THURSDAY	FRIDAY	SATURDAY

SUNDAY

DAILY PLAN

DATE .... S M T W T F S

SCHEDULE

7:00am	
7:30am	
8:00am	
8:30am	
9:00am	
9:30am	
10:00am	
10:30am	
11:00am	
11:30am	
12 noon	
12:30pm	
1:00pm	
1:30pm	
2:00pm	
2:30pm	
3:00pm	

TOP PRIORITIES

1
2
3
4
5

GRATITUDE

1
2
3
4
5

TO DO ✔ OK ➡ DELAY ✖ CANCEL

SLEEP DURATION & QUALITY

Hours: Mins:

HEALTH & FITNESS

WATER INTAKE

MEAL TRACKING

EXPENDITURE

NOTES

MOOD TODAY     

AFFIRMATIONS

I achieve everything I put my mind to
Success is the outcome of all that I do
I show up for myself daily
I am focused and consistent
I am strong and resilient

I will not stress over things I cannot control
I will have an excellent week full of possibilities and incredible opportunities
Each day brings new possibilities and experiences
I believe in myself and trust in my abilities

Everything is working out for my highest good
Out of this situation only good will come and I am safe

Money comes to me easily
Money comes to me fast
Money loves my company
When money comes, it lasts

Peace comes to me easily
Peace comes to me fast
Peace loves my company
When peace comes, it lasts

Joy comes to me easily
Joy comes to me fast
Joy loves my company
When joy comes, it lasts

Love comes to me easily
Love comes to me fast
Love loves my company
When love comes, it lasts

QUARTELY REVIEW ASSESSMENT AND FEEDBACK

ACTIVITY/TASK	DATE ASSIGNED

DATE COMPLETED	CHALLENGES ENCOUNTERED	MECHANISMS FOR OVERCOMING & AVOIDING FUTURE SIMILAR OCCURRENCES

BUILDING THE ACHIEVE MINDSET

MONTH	QUARTERLY AND MONTHLY REFLECTIONS FOR ACHIEVING CONSISTENTLY
1st Quarter Overlay	*"Start Where You Are. Use What You Have. Do What You Can." -* **Arthur Ashe**
January	*"By accepting responsibility for everything in your life, you create the power to change anything in your life." -* **Hal Elrod**
February	*"Sometimes the smallest step in the right direction ends up being the biggest step of your life. Tiptoe if you must, but take the step." -* **Naeem Callaway**
March	*Wake up every day with the expectation that something amazing is about to happen.*
2nd Quarter Overlay	*"I AM, two of the most powerful words for what you put after them shapes your reality." -* **Bevan Lee**
April	*"Each day is an adventure in discovering the meaning of life." -* **Jack Canfield**
May	*"Our very survival depends on our ability to stay awake, to adjust to new ideas, to remain vigilant and to face the challenge of change." -* **Martin Luther King Jr**
June	*Be grateful for every second of every day you get to spend with people you love. -* **Mandy Hale**
3rd Quarter Overlay	*"Obstacles don't have to stop you. If you run into a wall, don't turn around and give up. Figure out how to climb it, go through it, or work around it." -* **Michael Jordan**
July	*An amazing life does not just happen. It is created by prayer, kindness, hard work, humility and love.*
August	*You can learn anything if you have the courage to accept it and the intention to improve yourself.*
September	*"Don't let Anyone's ignorance, hate, drama or negativity stop you from being the best person you can be." -* **Dr Richard Munang**
4th Quarter Overlay	*Let people make incorrect assumptions about you, understand that their narrative has nothing to do with you, but is fuelled by their own fears and insecurities!*
October	*"Positive mindset brings positive things." -* **Phillip Reiter**
November	*"Be brave enough to face your own flaws, shortcomings and insecurities. Self-awareness is a super power." -* **Maria Joseph**
December	*"Don't imprison yourself in an echo chamber because oftentimes the opinion you don't want to hear, is the piece of advice you need most." -* **Maria Joseph**

WEEK	WEEKLY REFLECTIONS FOR ACHIEVING CONSISTENTLY
1	*"Don't be distracted by criticism. Remember, the only taste of success some people have is when they take a bite out of you." - **Zig Ziglar***
2	*Time is a real luxury which can never be purchased at any cost so make the most of it.*
3	*Choose to focus on positive, uplifting and happy thoughts because your inner world creates your outer world.*
4	*"Sometimes you have to go through the worst, to get to the best. Keep moving forward. Be patient." - **Karen Salmansohn***
5	*"Stop being afraid of what could go wrong and start being excited about what could go right." - **Tony Robbins***
6	*"The greatest inspiration you can ever get is to know that you are an inspiration to others. Wake up and start living an inspirational life." - **Steve Maraboli***
7	*Whatever life throws your way, strive to be better than you were yesterday, do better, choose better. Take tiny steps towards improvement. Love yourself enough to challenge your weakness with courage and allow yourself the strength to shift direction and change what is needed. Growth can be messy and hard, but so worth it in the end.*
8	*"The struggle you're in today is developing the strength you need for tomorrow. Don't give up." - **Robert Tew***
9	*"Insecurity is just an excuse to be lazy. Insecure about your weight then join a gym, insecure about your looks, get a make-over, insecure about your intelligence then read a book or take a class, emotionally unstable then start therapy. Confidence overcomes insecurity." - **Maria Joseph***
10	*"Never be bullied into silence. Never allow yourself to be made a victim. Accept no one's definition of your life; define yourself." - **Harvey Fierstein***
11	*"There is nothing more beautiful than someone who goes out of their way to make life beautiful for others." - **Mandy Hale***
12	*Be a blessing. Be a friend. Encourage someone. Take time to care without expectation!*

BUILDING THE ACHIEVE MINDSET

WEEK	WEEKLY REFLECTIONS FOR ACHIEVING CONSISTENTLY
13	*Appreciate where you are in your journey, even if it's not where you want to be. Every season serves a purpose.*
14	*Surround yourself with people who push you to be better. No jealousy, only positive energy, higher vibration and achieving your goals.*
15	*"Excuses are the nails used to build a house of failure." -* **Jim Rohn**
16	*"A bend in the road is not the end of the road unless you fail to make the turn." -* **Helen Keller**
17	*Be the person who dances in the flames of your pain and still send sparks out to light the way for others. –* **Trudi Jane**
18	*"We are not given a good life or a bad life. We are given a life. It's up to us to make it good or bad." -* **Ward Foley**
19	*Consistency builds confidence.*
20	*If you do not learn the difference between someone who is against you and someone who challenges you, you'll be pushing away nourishment for your soul to embrace those who will starve it.*
21	*Let your words heal, not wound. Remember, love and kindness are never wasted.*
22	*"Strength does not come from physical capacity. It comes from indomitable will."* **Mahatma Gandhi**
23	*"A meaningful life is not about being rich, being popular, being highly educated or being perfect. It's about being real, being humble, being able to share ourselves and touch the lives of others." -* **Samiksha Tekam**
24	*"You are magnificent beyond measure, perfect in your imperfections, and wonderfully made." -* **Abiola Abrams**

WEEK	WEEKLY REFLECTIONS FOR ACHIEVING CONSISTENTLY
25	*Accepting accountability for where you are now gives you the power to change your circumstances.*
26	*"Beautiful thoughts, build a beautiful soul."* - **Wayne W. Dyer**
27	*"Master patience, and you would have mastered everything."* - **George Savile**
28	*Do not stay in an unhealthy or unhappy situation to prove your loyalty. It's not worth the expense of your mental and emotional health and stability.*
29	*The past is in your head, but the future is in your hands.*
30	*"In addition to managing your time, you must manage your energy and focus to stay in control of how you use the willpower that you need, in order to become more productive."* - **Maria Joseph**
31	*"Opportunities are like the sunrise. If you wait too long, you miss them."* **William Arthur Ward**
32	*Difficult does not mean impossible. It only means that you have to work hard.* - **J R Dilip**
33	*Take some time to appreciate the precious gift of life and Give Thanks. Be kind, positive and let love be your guide.*
34	*"Do not complain about others, change yourself if you want peace because it's easier to protect your feet with slippers than to carpet the whole world."* **Anthony de Mello**
35	*"Love yourself-accept yourself, forgive yourself and be good to yourself, because without you the rest of us are without a source of many wonderful things."* **Leo Buscaglia**
36	*The bad times in our life often takes us exactly where we need to be to experience our best life.*

BUILDING THE ACHIEVE MINDSET

WEEK	WEEKLY REFLECTIONS FOR ACHIEVING CONSISTENTLY
37	*"Vision is the art of seeing what is invisible to others." - **Jonathan Smith***
38	*"Your mindset is your BIGGEST asset. Care for it as such." - **Maria Joseph***
39	*You are not always in control. Life is full of experiences, lessons, heartbreaks and pain, but it is also filled with love, beauty and new beginnings, embrace it all. It makes us who we are, and after every storm comes a clear sky.*
40	*Embrace your suffering and adversity for it builds character, and greatness comes from character.*
41	*"The best thing you could do is master the chaos in you, you are not thrown into the Fire. You are the fire." - **Mama Indigo***
42	*This is your weekly reminder that you are amazing and you can handle anything!*
43	*Health does not always come from food we eat, supplements or sun, but from peace of mind, peace of heart and peace of soul. It also comes from your laughter and love.*
44	*Life is temporary so problems can never be permanent. Find the solution!*
45	*What we desire is not always what we get... but unknowingly many times we get things much more than what we expect...These are called "Blessings." – **Ravindra Singh Thakur***
46	*Everything in your life is a reflection of a choice you once made, if you want different results make different choices.*
47	*"Real isn't who is with you at your celebration. Real is who is standing next to you at rock bottom." - **Trent Shelton***
48	*"You are your greatest asset, your best tool and your fastest vehicle in getting to exactly where you want to go so use your energy wisely." - **Maria Joseph***

*"Focus on the 24 hours in front of you and do what you can to get closer to where you want to be."- **Eric Thomas***

Let the rising of the sun every morning remind us to be thankful for everything we have in life.

Rest tonight, knowing whatever is on your mind is in God's hands.

*"We rise by lifting others." - **Robert Ingersoll***

Look forward to the miracles that await you today.

Never underestimate the skill of listening, practise it frequently.

*"There is no such thing as a perfect moment, just take a moment and make it perfect." - **Aryn Kyle***

Embrace difficulty and challenges and overcome them with Grace and poise, because adversity builds strength of character.

Whatever you decide to do, make sure it brings a smile to your face and joy to your heart, even if the smile and joy come only in the long run.

*You do not have to prove anything to anyone. It is wonderful to be alive, to be who you are and to grow; ultimately that's all that matters. - **Sadhguru***

One kind word can change someone's whole day so say the things you want to hear.

*"95% of problems in life are due to the tone of our voice. It's not what we say, it's how we say it. Just change the tone and see the change in life." - **Hazique Shadon***

BUILDING THE ACHIEVE MINDSET

"No one is perfect. We all make mistakes we all say wrong things we do wrong things we fall we get up we learn we grow we move on we live and we thank God for always giving us another chance." - **Helen Barry**

Take life day by day and be grateful for the little things. Don't get stressed over what you can't control. "Consistency will take you beyond motivation, stay the course! - **Maria Joseph**

"Time alone can prove the worth of people in our lives, not everyone is meant to be in our lives...As time goes by, the wrong ones disappear and the best ones remain forever." - **Bhola Das**

"Time is still the best answer, forgiveness is still the best painkiller, and God is still the best healer." – **Shaune B Ryder**

Make the most of this day being present in every moment.

Before you assume - learn the facts.
Before you judge - understand why.
Before you speak - think.

Acquiring knowledge and learning new skills increases your efficiency. Stay committed! - **Maria Joseph**

"Calmness is a human super power. The ability not to overreact or take things personally keeps your mind, clear and heart of peace." **Darren Weissman**

"When you believe every breath is a gift, you take nothing for granted." – **Invajy**

No matter where life leads, be good and grateful to the people around you. Every single person has been strategically placed in your life at the perfect moment for a reason. Perhaps you are to learn a lesson, have someone strengthen your courage, your knowledge or face your emotions, whatever it may be, even if only for a moment, you can be certain that there is a reason!

"Meditation and prayer are important but how we treat others after we pray is more important." - **Vishal Badole**

Every adversity, difficulty, challenge, and obstacle comes with a hidden blessing.

"When you do something beautiful, and nobody notices, do not be sad for every morning the sun is a beautiful spectacle, and yet most of the audience sleeps in." - **John Lennon**

Decrease your circle in size but increase it in value.

"Do not ignore the message just because you dislike the messenger. Often the voices we perceive as mean, that trigger us or tell us the things we don't want to hear are the voices and advice we most need to level up." - **Maria Joseph**

You are loved by God. Do not surrender your circumstances. Even on days you feel weak or struggle, God is always there. His unconditional love will give you the strength to continue.

NEVER be afraid to share what you know.
"To teach is to learn twice over." - **Joseph Joubert**

"Believe in yourself by honouring your instincts and trusting your intuition." - **Maria Joseph**

Today, I am ready to receive all the blessings that the universe will bestow on me.

"Obstacles are opportunities in disguise." - **Deepak Chopra**

As flowers open with fresh scents in the mornings, so does the hand of God with new blessings. May you receive them today and always.

There are only two ways to be happy, change your situation or change your mindset toward it.

The greatest treasure on earth are the people who love and support us, they cannot be bought or replaced and each of us have only a few of them.

Love requires action. Trust necessitates proof. Sorry entails change!

BUILDING THE ACHIEVE MINDSET

REFLECTIONS FOR BEING PRESENT

We always work for a better tomorrow, but when tomorrow comes instead of enjoying, we think of a better tomorrow! Let's have a better today!

Nothing is as nice as having someone who appreciates you in the smallest things, accepts you in times of hardship, comforts you when you are troubled, loves you no matter what and is simply happy for having you in their life. Go be that person!

"Listen with curiosity, speak with honesty and act with integrity." **Roy T Bennett**

"Lessons learned from failure, often build the character we need to climb to the next level." - **Maria Joseph**

Life is never easy. We have to make it easy sometimes by ignoring something and sometimes by accepting something.

The moments that we think are meant to break us, are meant to evolve and transform us into the persons we are meant to be, and into our purpose.

Another day, another experience, be grateful.

"Every phase in our life is meant to teach us something valuable. It depends on us whether we analyse the lessons or just turn the pages." - **Sahil Sathe**

Focus on what you have and you will have more, concentrate on what you don't have and you will never be content.

Don't get so caught up in where you want to be that you forget how far you've come. Celebrate the small milestones and wins for they will provide you with nourishment to keep you going.

"Be prepared to either have difficult conversations or to live a difficult life." - **Maria Joseph**

Stop wasting precious time and positive energy worrying about the things you cannot change.

REFLECTIONS FOR BUILDING CONFIDENCE

"Time is priceless. You can't own it, but you can use it. You can't keep it, but you can spend it. Once you have lost it, you can never get it back."
Harvey Mac Kay

Your feelings are always valid, you behaviour however may not be, so don't act on your feelings.

Using someone else's ruler to measure your self-worth will always leave you short.

"Power and people pleasing are directly opposed to each other. Choose the type of person you want to be and the type of life you want to live." -
Maria Joseph

Excellence is a choice and there are absolutely no shortcuts.

When things don't go as planned, change your plan to align with the resources and opportunities currently available to you.

We all have a past, we all made choices that were not the best ones. None of us are completely innocent, but we get a fresh start every day to be a better person than we were yesterday.

"Time qualifies all things under the sun. The villain of today's story is often viewed as tomorrow's hero. Stay true to yourself and always do what you know to be right." -
Maria Joseph

"Family isn't always blood. It's the people in your life who want you in theirs. The ones who accept you for who you are. The ones who would do anything to see you smile, and who love you no matter what." **- Maya Angelou**

We don't know what tomorrow will bring so don't stay angry for too long. Learn to forgive and love with all your heart.

"Someone else's lack of planning should never constitute an emergency on your part. "NO" is a complete sentence! Stay Focused!" - **Maria Joseph**

Never be a prisoner of your past. It was just a lesson, not a life sentence.

BUILDING THE ACHIEVE MINDSET

*"If you don't go after what you want, you'll never have it. If you don't ask, the answer's always no, if you don't step forward you're always in the same place." - **Nora Roberts***

Many small choices will eventually put you in a good place... choose wisely.

"What we know matters, but who we are matters more." Brene Brown

View your problems as blessings in disguise and that's exactly what they will become.

Grace is when God gives us good things that we don't deserve. Mercy is when he spares us from bad things we deserve. Blessings are when he is generous with both.

*"Surrounding yourself with different perspectives will expand your mind. Discomfort builds development!" - **Maria Joseph***

It was what it was. It is what it is. It will be what it will be. You may not be able to control every situation, but you are able to control how it affects you. Nothing is worth sacrificing your peace of mind.

*"Betrayal is inevitable for even Jesus was betrayed...build resilience!" - **Maria Joseph***

Release that which does not serve you or align with your higher purpose or future self.

*"Keep the faith. Some of life's most amazing things happen when you're about to give up." - **Helen Barry***

Regardless of what you face, you are backed by God!

Stop overthinking! Instead close your eyes and think of those who never had a chance to open their eyes ever again. Now go fulfil the purpose for which you are on this earth.

www.ingramcontent.com/pod-product-compliance
Lightning Source LLC
Chambersburg PA
CBHW040906110726
48005CB00006B/817